"Everyone has a past, but our past does not have to define who we are today and who we'll be in the future."
- unknown

IN THE DARK

A Mother's Reflections on her
Son's Addiction and Recovery

Nancy Kuykendall

IN THE DARK

A Mother's Reflections on Her Son's Addiction and
Recovery

by

Nancy Kuykendall

Copyright © 2024

No names are used except for the subject of the book – with his permission.

Editing – Mike Unrue

Formatting – Nancy Kuykendall

Cover Photo – stock photo - Pixabay

Cover Design – Waqar Nadeem at BookBosss

ACKNOWLEDGEMENTS

Thank you, Mike, author J.M. Unrue, for your editing skills and being willing to tackle a new project. You are needed and appreciated. I've enjoyed our sharing and working together.

Thank you, Kaira, author Kaira Lockwood, for your encouragement and camaraderie. Our discussions are helpful, and fun. I look forward to our talks and all that we learn together in this work and joy of authorship.

Thank you, Estella, author Estella Boger, for your friendship and our time spent together. I look forward to and enjoy our tea-time chats and book talk as we explore authorship together.

Thank you, Mr. Waqar Nadeem for your excellent work in book cover design. Your multiple skills are invaluable.

Thank you, Jason, for suggesting I write this book, for continually urging me to write it, and most of all for your recovery. Your courage and determination are remarkable. You are a hero.

Thank you, my husband Steve, for your constant love and support in all I do. You know me so well. What would I do without you?

Thank you, Lord God, for sustaining me during dark times, for saving Jason, and for helping me get my thoughts together enough to write this book.

With Gratitude,
Nancy

For Jason

Dedicated

to

Mothers

CONTENTS

Preface

In the dark, is exactly where I was when my oldest child, Jason, first experimented with addictive substances and displayed addictive behavior. To my recollection he was only twelve years old at the first signs of impending trouble. He remembers it as ten-years-old. That's far too young to be introduced to drugs. My gut feelings told me things were not right, but I didn't know exactly from where those feelings stemmed. I was dealing with a troubled marriage on top of Jason's issues. Jason, like me at the time, tended to keep his feelings stuffed inside. That's never a good thing.

I grew up in a home where I never saw cigarettes, alcohol, or drugs of any kind. There was no swearing or abuse. My dad was both a medical doctor working in pediatric hospitals and clinics, and a minister who was a seminary professor until he retired. I was surrounded by physicians who were interested in health and healthy ways of living and ministers and pastors who were doing their best to teach spiritual health through the Bible and God's ways. My mom was a stay-at-home mom who excelled in many forms of homemaking and took care of everyone's needs, often sacrificing her own. I raised my children in the same type of home and environment.

I have never smoked a cigarette, smoked marijuana, never once smoked, injected, snuffed, or huffed any drug. I've never had a beer, nor wine, nor hard liquor. I once let champagne touch my lips to taste it, but I've never drunk champagne. I have never purchased alcohol. I've never once been offered a drug. To be one hundred percent honest, around 1990 a friend gifted my husband (at the time) and I a four-pack of wine coolers. On two sizzling hot summer nights, home alone, and the kids in bed, I drank an eight-ounce glass of berry wine cooler over ice. It tasted nice enough. It was refreshing, but I didn't like the feeling of alcohol in my body. Long story short, I'd decided at age fourteen to never drink. I wanted to keep that promise I'd made to myself. Since those wine coolers, I've never had alcohol again.

I was completely naive about drugs and drug abuse. I was unaware of behaviors that might be tell-tale signs. I was *in the dark* when it came to understanding what might be going on with my son. I understood some of the problems he had, and I understood his "stuff it" personality.

I loved him fiercely.

One day Jason ran away. For me that's where the story begins. This book is written to express my journey through Jason's addiction, and then recovery. It took twenty years. Jason's first day of sobriety was December 6, 2012. He has been clean and sober ever since. I am a grateful Mom!

Jason first urged me to write this book ten years ago, and to write it from my perspective as his mother. He told me, "The book is not about me, Mom. It's about you." But in so many ways for me it is about Jason. A mother's child is a part of her forever.

This book is not one long account of twenty years. My knowledge of all that went on is sketchy and my memories are scattered and sometimes vague. Dates and details may not be fully accurate in every case. My approach is to relate episodes and experiences I remember. The purpose of this book, as Jason and I both hope, is to help other mothers know they are not alone and how to have hope and persist while knowing that any day word might come that their precious son or daughter is dead.

I hope that my experiences, as best as I can remember them, will help other mothers. My prayers were many. My faith grew stronger, and hope lived in my heart. My love for Jason was and is beyond measure, as it is for my other two children as well. Love is a strong conqueror—a mother's fierce love, but even more so, Almighty God's powerful and compassionate love. I am a fortunate mother to have a drug-free son still with me today. Not everyone's child makes it out alive.

We do our best to love and raise our children, but there are no perfect parents, nor perfect children. We parents often have our own struggles. We train our children to the best of our abilities and sometimes still lose them by their own choices. Mothers are not automatically at fault. I know I did my very best, no matter how *in the dark* I was. I sometimes remember moments that still hurt my heart terribly that I wish I had handled differently.

I was a young inexperienced mom, and I wish I hadn't listened to all the well-meaning advice I was given ... even by some doctors. We can "if only" or "I wish" but it serves no purpose. We can't change the past. We can't change our children's choices. Circumstances were difficult for me, but I loved my children deeply, with all my heart, and know I did my very best raising them. Because of that, I have given myself the gift of grace. Long ago, before I was ever married or a mother, I accepted God's compassionate grace, and he has seen me through rough waters with love, forgiveness, and hope. I am free of guilt. I hope you are, too.

With love,
Nancy

"There is no force on earth more powerful than a mother's love."

1

WHERE'S JASON

It was the summer of 1991. If memory serves it was on or near the fourth of July and we'd planned a rare family gathering at our house. My mother had passed away the previous August and my dad was driving down to our home in the San Joaquin Valley of California from his home just north of the San Francisco Bay Area. Coming with him were my brother and his wife and one of my sisters. Family didn't come our way all that often and I had been preparing the house and yard and food for their visit. They would be staying just for the day. A long drive down and back for them.

It was going to be sizzling hot, as was the norm in our summers. We had our twenty-four-foot, four feet deep, above-ground pool clean and ready for cooling off. We planned to grill burgers and hotdogs, and I had all the picnic side dishes ready. The five of us were eagerly awaiting my family's arrival. This was in the days before cell phones. I knew when my dad planned to arrive, but there was no communication during their travel. We would watch and wait.

My kids were getting up slowly. When Jason didn't appear, I went to roust him. I entered the room he and his younger brother shared, but he wasn't in his bed. I knew I hadn't seen him come into the kitchen—the first room he would have entered after coming down the hallway and through the entryway. A feeling of dread shadowed over me as I walked to the side of his bed. My throat tightened and I held my breath. There was a note. My heart began to pound.

There in Jason's handwriting were the words, *'I'm not coming home.'* My stomach lurched and my knees went weak as I fought off the panic. *'Where did he go?'* my mind screamed. He was only twelve years old. I hurried to both his brother and sister, ages ten and seven, and asked if they had seen Jason or knew where he was? Both answered, "No."

None of us had a clue where Jason had gone, or when he'd left. I imagined he had sneaked out during the very early morning hours. I didn't know why, but I knew he'd been troubled. I knew his spirit had been squelched multiple times over. This stemmed partly from at least two times in his life that came to mind, and it sickened and concerned me. I had felt his pain more than once. I had little control in those matters, though I had stood up for Jason. If I had known then what I know now, or if I'd been older, wiser, and stronger maybe I could have done more.

I immediately began calling the mothers of his closest friends. They had not seen Jason but promised to keep an eye out. My husband and I took both cars and began driving around our neighborhood. We lived in the rural outskirts of the city proper. There was a lot of area to search. Soon, I remembered I had family arriving and I had to be there to welcome them. I felt I had to put on a happy face and act as normally as possible. Looking back now, I wonder why I felt that way. I was screaming inside to find my son. I should have been able to fall into my family's arms when they arrived and tell them the situation and received their help. I was afraid to tell them. I didn't always feel emotionally safe with family, and I felt like an utter failure that my son had run away from home. I believe the way I acted did not allow my family to know the gravity of the situation. Even as we swam and ate, I was continually listening for the phone and making more calls. I needed to find Jason and forget the niceties. Jason was in pain, and so was his Momma. I continued to straddle an incomprehensible fence of entertaining and finding my missing son.

Finally, a call came from a woman I knew through our church. She'd seen Jason walking down the country road that led to her home, thought it odd, stopped, spoke to him, and invited him to go to her house. He knew her and went with her. I didn't know, or maybe don't remember, the conversation she'd had with Jason, but he allowed her to call me saying he'd talk with me only. She and I spoke briefly then she put Jason on the phone. My first words were, "Are you okay?" I don't remember his response. I asked, "Will you come home?" He didn't want to. He didn't want to be around or face his dad. I don't know what the precipitating factor was that caused him to leave, but he wanted nothing to do with his dad at that moment. I asked him if I could come pick him up if I came alone. He finally agreed and relief flooded through my body and mind.

I felt a great sense of urgency to go get Jason immediately. I told my husband, my other two children, and my visiting family that Jason had been found and would come home if I went alone to pick him up. I needed to leave the gathering to go get him. My dad decided that they should all leave, seeing that we had a lot to deal with. They would leave and let us handle our situation. In mere minutes they were gone.

Part of me felt abandoned and part of me felt relieved. I didn't think a lot about this until I began writing this book. In retrospect, I do feel I was abandoned. Looking back, wouldn't it have been a great reassurance to Jason, and all of us, if they had stayed and welcomed him home with open arms, and expressing their concern? It has been suggested that Jason probably left that very day— knowing family was coming—as a loud cry for help. He needed extra help. Now it was up to me to get to the bottom of his most pressing problems.

I sped off to get my hurting son. I desperately wanted him to know how loved and wanted he was. I wanted to heal his broken spirit. I yearned to soothe his pain. How would I do this? First, I needed to get him home.

Jason willingly got into the car. He saw I'd kept my word and had come alone, and I believe he trusted me. I talked to him gently on the drive home. I told him I was going to help him. I told him this very afternoon he would have his say with no retribution. It was his turn to talk and be heard. I promised him I'd handle it when we got home, and he would be able to talk freely. The fear I felt began to shift to anger and protectiveness. The "mother bear" was rising within and I would protect!

When we arrived home, Jason sheepishly walked into the house. He didn't know what to expect. I told him family had left and I began to take charge over everyone and everything. I sent the other two kids out to play. Once they were situated, I continued to take charge. I surprised myself by how I took over. I told my husband not to say a word. We had an oval kitchen table and I asked Jason to sit at one end and asked his dad to sit at the other. I would sit in the middle and act as mediator; neither of them was to talk unless I allowed it. Jason did as I asked and sat meekly. His dad sat at the other end without speaking. I was relieved by their compliance.

It was my intention to let Jason speak without interruption or correction from either of us. I told him he was free to speak his mind and share his feelings, and neither his dad nor I would interject. I shot his dad a look hoping he'd agree and stay silent until his turn to speak. I intensely wanted Jason to feel free to share. He was finally getting a chance. It wasn't easy though. He couldn't bring himself to speak the words locked inside. I watched him struggle and finally asked if I might help him by asking a few questions. I figured it would give him a clear place to start. I asked him if he wanted to share what had upset him enough to run away? Could he tell us? He stumbled around. I asked him if he felt uneasy telling us and if he felt he wasn't heard? Mostly, I asked him to share his feelings.

It was extremely difficult for him to do so and not a lot was said. Eventually, it came time for his dad to speak. What Jason said and what his dad said are a blur to me now. All I truly remember is that I went to bed that night knowing all was not well. The problem wasn't solved. Not enough had been said and nothing had been rectified. My heart ached and I was concerned.

I understood Jason's uneasiness from several angles. I dealt with not being able to express myself well, or freely, in my marriage and within my family. Though I had some sense of uneasiness with them and felt abandonment, I also know that if I'd been able to say what I needed to, and explain more what was happening, and shared my feelings and concerns, my family might have stayed and tried to help. What I did know, as I learned more as time went on, is that when a person speaks up but is shot down, or speaks up and their voice goes unheard, and feelings are nullified, they will shut down. This is a dangerous way to live. People will turn to all kinds of things to ease their pain. Easing emotional pain with drugs and alcohol is one way. A deadly way. An all-too-common way.

2

THE FIRST SIGNS

T he sun had set and it was growing dark. I checked on the kids to make sure they were inside and all was well. It was time to start settling in for the night. I couldn't find Jason. I called out to him around the house and our large backyard. I didn't see him or hear a reply. I looked out the large bay window in the kitchen that faced the front yard, and by the road saw a tiny glimmer of light. I took a long look, not sure what I was seeing. Soon, I began to see Jason's faint form standing next to the mailbox at the end of our driveway. What was that light? What was he doing? Why hadn't he answered me or come in?'

Then I realized, he was hiding out to smoke a cig-arette. Where did my twelve-year-old son get a ciga-rette? And when? When did he start smoking? That all-too-familiar heart pounding and lurching stomach visited me again. My young son was smoking dirty and dangerous cigarettes. That was not okay with me.

Worry, tinged with anger, propelled me outside to confront Jason. I wanted to know why he was smoking. His answer was he wanted to. I wanted to know where he got the cigarettes. He wasn't telling. I told him to drop it, put it out, and come inside to get ready for bed. He did as I asked but in no big hurry. I ushered him inside the house.

I didn't know it then, but that was the first sign of what would become years of drug addiction. He once told me that quitting cigarettes was the hardest of all. After he'd gotten clean and sober, he fought his cigarette addiction for a long while until he finally conquered it, too. Jason had exercise-induced asthma, first diagnosed when he was a small boy. He struggled with asthma and used inhalers but continued to smoke. I could not understand such behavior, but cigarettes are extremely addicting as so many people know.

Jason remembers an experience that I do not. He asked me if I remember when he was ten years old, and a neighbor called to inform me that he was smoking. He says he was brought inside, and I held him and loved on him and kept hugging him. He doesn't remember anything said by his father or me, but he remembers me lovingly holding him. I'm glad he has that memory because it means something to him. I'm glad I reacted that way though I do not remember it. I'm sure I just wanted to make everything okay. We might believe that if we love someone enough all problems will be conquered and disappear. It's not true. We can love greatly and others will still make their own choices—sometimes detrimental choices.

Jason was a sweet and quiet little boy. He played like all little kids, and I had a lot of fun playing with him, showing him things, and teaching him. I'll never forget the day he was a tiny little boy sitting in his car seat, pointed to the sky, and said, "bird". I looked up and saw the bird. I became so excited that he had put that together—recognized a bird and called it by name. I was a stay-at-home mom and fully enjoyed my role as a mother.

Jason also exhibited a stubborn side to his personality that at times greatly challenged me. I tried to listen to my heart for what was right when disciplining him, but I was given unwanted advice that often confused me. Those who had been parents longer than I wanted to tell me how to handle things. I listened but didn't necessarily agree with their ideas or appreciate their input. I respected these parents but not all children or situations are the same. So many of the discipline decisions were left to me. Though I was married, I was home alone days and often into the evenings. By then Jason was asleep.

One of my biggest challenges was bedtime. At one month of age, we took Jason to meet his grandpa. My mom had come to stay a week when Jason was born, but my dad, a pediatrician, who had not laid eyes on him yet and was eager to check him over. It was a joyful time having Jason with his grandparents until I put him down for the night. There was a crib for him in my parent's room that they had given us to use while we were there. I had nursed Jason and rocked him to sleep, but soon after he was put in the crib he woke and began to cry. His cries became what sounded like panic. He was in a new environment—maybe it scared him. I went to him, soothed him, and he quieted down. Soon, however, he was crying hysterically again. My husband, my dad, and my mom all took a turn trying to quiet him. It didn't work. I went to him one more time and then insisted everyone stay out of the room and leave him be. It was a horrible time until he finally cried himself out and slept. Was this the right thing to do? I still have no idea. I have since read that children will cry out of anger that can be mistaken as fear or pain. Even small children can manipulate their parents with anger. Different types of cries have been documented through medical and psychological testing. Very young children can use anger against their unsuspecting parents who might be struggling to know how to handle certain situations. I don't know what one month-old Jason was feeling. Ideas on parenting have changed over the decades. Some for the better; some for the worse. We parents wade through every crisis the best we can.

For a period, when Jason was around two, he simply would not stay in bed. By that time of day, I was tired and at a loss what to do with him. I rocked him, lay down with him, sang to him, and rubbed his back until he was asleep. Soon, however, he'd be up again, peeking around the corner at me. Nothing kept him in bed. At one point I sought our pediatrician's help. His advice was to put Jason to bed gently with the songs and rocking and back rubbing, etc., then lock his door from the outside so he could not come out. He also said to remove the light bulbs or unscrew them part way to make sure he could not turn a light on. He said no matter what Jason did to not go in or acknowledge him. I tried this once. Jason screamed and cried. He sounded like a hysterical trapped animal. When he finally fell quiet, and I thought he was asleep, I went into his room to check on him. As I approached his bed and saw his tear-stained face my heart broke. He woke suddenly, sat up and started crying, begging me not to do that again. I held him and said I would not, but he needed to stay in his bed. I lay with him, and he fell asleep.

The horror of hearing him cry and scream in terror undid me. I had paced and cried almost as hard as he did. I decided I could not, and would not, follow the doctor's advice and never do that again. As I recollect, Jason began staying in bed. Maybe the tactic worked. Just writing these accounts creates an awful feeling in my gut and tears fill my eyes. I wish I had been all knowing, and that Jason had been easier at bedtime, but neither were true. These are things moms deal with, stress over, and feel guilty about. At every age children can be challenging.

Jason was a good boy and mostly compliant and obedient. He would sometimes resist authority. I was excited the day he entered kindergarten. I thought he'd have so much fun. By then his brother and sister had been born. His brother was three and his sister was a baby. The three of us took Jason to kindergarten on his first day. I pushed a stroller while we walked since the school was only two-and-a-half blocks down the street.

Jason did well, but by the time first grade arrived the teachers were advising that he go instead to pre-first. It was a new program and a class developed for children who could graduate kindergarten but were considered not ready for first grade. There was one teacher who strongly supported the pre-first program and wanted to meet with us, asking that we bring Jason along for the interview. Jason immediately turned stubborn and no matter what the teacher asked, he refused to answer. He would not tell her his name, or if he had brothers and sisters, or pets. He would not answer the simplest questions, all of which he knew the answer, but stubbornly would not open his mouth.

I sat quietly in horror. The teacher took his silence as further proof he needed the pre-first class. Maybe she was right. She went on to tell us that there was strong evidence that kids who are pushed too soon or too quickly through school often end up with problems, drug addiction, and legal trouble. I listened, growing more horrified by the minute. Jason's dad was adamantly against the pre-first program and wanted him to enter first grade. I was undecided and needed time to think about it. By a certain date we were to let this teacher know our decision. I asked Jason why he wouldn't answer the questions. He didn't want to, that's why.

As Jason grew and we faced additional issues, I learned that if someone in authority wanted Jason to do something he would rebel, simply because they wanted him to do it. As far as going into first grade, I wanted him to move up with his friends, but was concerned for his overall well-being. His dad remained against Jason going into pre-first and Jason entered first grade. At first his teacher—a very loving woman—was concerned about Jason and thought he might need to go back, but by week four, she called again to say he was doing fine, and she believed he'd do well in first grade. He stayed in her class. Her words brought me some much-needed relief and peace-of-mind.

Looking back years later, I wondered if the reason he fell into drugs and other difficulties was because he had been unprepared for first grade.

Jason continued smoking and I continued to try to find out where he got his cigarettes. I wasn't sure if he got them from other kids' parents, had older kids buy them for him, or if the local convenience store employees ignored the rules, including alcohol. All three possibilities made me livid.

One afternoon, I knew Jason had snuck off with friends to smoke and do who knows what else. I was still a stay-at-home mom, but all the while my kids were growing up, I taught piano lessons in our home most afternoons. It would soon be time to teach, and I needed to know where the kids were and make sure they were home, or playing at a friend's home where there was some supervision. I don't remember how I knew where Jason had likely gone, but I drove to one of his friend's homes knowing the parents were at work and the boys would be alone in the house. When I arrived, I knocked lightly on the door. When I received no answer, I tried the door, found it unlocked and walked in. I was a mom on the warpath and I fully intended to find my son and jerk him out of there. He was at least thirteen or fourteen at the time but needed supervision because of his attitude and poor choices.

I heard voices and followed the sound. I soon discovered a group of boys in the garage. The door was partly open and I saw Jason sitting on the washer, his back to me, and a group of boys standing in front of him hanging on his every word. He was smoking and talking to them as if he was the leader of the group. I quietly pushed the door open further. The boys facing Jason saw me, went quiet, and turned pale. They were staring at me and Jason soon realized that something was up. He turned and saw me. He knew he was busted. I went to him, took his arm, and ordered him to come with me. I was sad and angry all at once. I took him to the car and told him I was taking him to his dad who would watch him the rest of the day while I taught my students. His dad was not only the pastor in our community (which only made our situation worse) but also worked as a real estate agent. He was at the real estate office and that's where I took Jason. He was not happy about the arrangement, but I told him since he couldn't be trusted, he would be supervised all afternoon.

I went inside the office with Jason to tell his dad what was up, and that Jason needed to stay with him while I was teaching. I left. This was one of the first times that I had to find a way to concentrate on my students and teach them well while my mind was elsewhere. We needed the income. Teaching provided grocery money to feed our family. It was necessary, yet terribly difficult when my wayward son was constantly on my mind. For the moment, the immediate problem was solved.

3

Night Excursions

Though I never did it myself, it seems it's some kind of right-of-passage for many teens that they sneak out at night. They make their escape out front and back doors never being heard, or more likely crawl out their bedroom windows. Most often they meet up with other nocturnal escapees while unsuspecting parents sleep. I never heard any of my kids slip out, but I believe they each participated in those night activities at least a few times. Jason, being the oldest, may have begun this activity alone. I have no idea, but I eventually became aware of the excursions. He and his brother, sharing a room, slept in the largest bedroom at the back of the house. Not only did they have a good-sized window, but French doors that opened onto our screened-in patio—an easy getaway. I just never dreamed one or both would go running around during the dark of night. Again, my naivete. Boys would meet up and Jason was out there with them. I eventually learned girls were running around in the wee hours as well. I didn't find it funny. I found it dangerous and disobedient. I already knew that alcohol and cigarettes, at the least, were on the menu of their so-called fun. Discovering these escapades—I believe from another mother—I became angrily vigilant.

One night, when I'd had a heads-up an escape was planned, I locked the French doors and hid the key, and made a makeshift lock and trap by the window—something that would make noise. I gathered up my sleeping bag and some padding to go underneath to soften the tile floor, took my pillow, and camped out in the small foyer in front of the dead-bolted front door. To get to that door, or to the back door, Jason, would have to step over me. Not knowing I was there, he'd likely trip. I was concerned about taking the key out of the front door, having already locked the bedroom and the back doors. Without a key in the doors, escaping a fire would be much more difficult. We didn't have a good plan, but it had never been an issue before. Once innocence disappeared everything became difficult.

I lay on the hard floor all night listening and waiting. I never heard a sound, and nothing happened. I thought I might catch Jason and maybe other boys waiting outside, in the act, but I think my trap was discovered. At least he'd stayed in the house safe and sound that night—as far as I knew. I certainly couldn't sleep on the foyer floor or stay awake every night, so that plan ended rather abruptly, but I became more diligent checking on all three kids multiple times a night. I was concerned for their safety and the trouble they could get into.

I can't remember exactly what time frame this happened, but one night I heard noise coming from our backyard patio. My tendency when I hear strange noises, both then and now, is to go look. If our dog was barking, I'd go check out the situation. In these cases, fear was not my first reaction. Curiosity, concern, and even anger came first. Though I slept well, I was also the one who woke most easily, so I was the one up checking the situation. Usually there was nothing to be concerned about, but that night I found a young man—an older teen—pacing around the back patio. He appeared to be under the influence, yet at the same time harmless. He looked familiar. Back in those days it wasn't so odd to open your door to a stranger and I did just that and had him come inside. I wouldn't do that today.

My husband either woke up or I woke him up, and came into the room. He knew the boy's dad, as did I, once I realized who the boy was. We called the father and he came to fetch his wayward, night wandering, drug using son. He was grateful and apologetic and sad. I felt great sorrow for that dad and the situation. I didn't know then that Jason would become just like him in time. It was a heartbreaking night. I never knew what became of that boy, but I have learned through the years of other boys my kids hung around with who died from drug use. It hurts my heart, even now, to think of the trap those boys fell into. I remember those young boys being over at our house, hanging out, and eating with us. I remember seeing them in my kids' classrooms. They were just kids, as Jason was, yet they were getting their hands on, and experimenting with, dangerous substances they should have never seen or been privy to.

Where did they get them? Who gave them to them, or where did the money come from? How many dope pushers were in our rural neighborhood? How many parents were using and stashing their paraphernalia, drugs, alcohol, and cigarettes in places the kids were able to snoop and find? I wanted to know how and where and who was aiding these young kids.

4

IN SEARCH OF THE ABBETORS

I had little luck finding those who were supplying drugs to the kids, but it didn't stop me from seeking an answer. There was one family I suspected but I had no proof. I suspected that one mom and dad had a hidden stash—of who knows what—that the boys found. Jason spent time at that home. Many of the families had working moms and dads and their teens were home alone after school. It was in one of those homes where I had found Jason happily smoking, as top dog, in front of his followers while sitting on the family washing machine.

I was one of the few stay-at-home moms, so I'm sure less happened at our house because I was there. Even when teaching, I was aware of who was at the house and relatively aware of what was going on. I made a point to know what was going on once I wised up to the situation. Also, we had no alcohol, cigarettes, or illegal drugs in our home. There was nothing to sneak except extra cookies. That, I didn't mind. Even now, I wonder why these kids were so keen on getting their hands on those illegal and dangerous substances. It was during the time that there was the push against drug use and Nancy Regan's 'SAY NO TO DRUGS' campaign was active. The schools and police were actively teaching against drug use. They clearly taught that one try and you can become hooked and travel down the dark path of addiction. Maybe all the attention given to drugs spurred curiosity. When I was their age, lessons I received at school and home were enough to scare me from ever wanting to touch any of it. But times had changed.

One day, in my fury to catch a convenience store owner who was suspected of supplying the kids with cigarettes, I stomped over to the store. It was only a few blocks away. I had no car at the time, and I liked to walk anyway. Power-walking to the store fueled my anger with every step. When I entered the store, hot and sweaty and worked up, I saw a gentleman working the counter. I had no idea if he was the owner, or an employee, but he was on the receiving end of my semi-controlled wrath. I told him point blank that he was suspected of giving underage teens cigarettes and alcohol and maybe worse. I asked him if he was doing this and told him if I caught him or anyone else in the act, I'd have the police there as fast as possible. I let him know I, and other moms, had no fear of staking out the store when they'd least expect it and turn them in the minute we saw anything suspicious.

He denied any involvement with supplying the kids, of course, but I didn't believe him and told him so. I'm not sure if he'd had an irate mom in his face before, but he did that day. Though I went there alone to confront that store owner, I knew a few other moms who were upset. I made myself and the other moms sound as scary and fierce as I could, but I doubt it unsettled that man. He probably had a good laugh when I left. Still, I did watch that store when I thought kids might be there. I frequented it more often so I could scope things out, but I had my two younger kids to watch, piano students to teach, dinner to make, and so on. I needed a private detective, but that was unaffordable. I wish now I'd found a way to hire one. I truly do.

Sneaky and elusive behavior continued from Jason. There was nothing concrete that I found and nothing concrete to call the police about. I did talk to them, but as is the case, the offender would have to be caught in the act. I asked the police to keep an eye on the store, but I don't know if they did. So, I watched my son. Things felt 'off' but I didn't know enough to put my finger on anything. Jason was attending school and doing okay for the moment. He was outwardly obedient and did his chores, but whenever he left who knows what transpired.

Jason wasn't a bad boy. He's never been inherently 'bad' but when a kid makes poor choices bad things can happen. I think, at the time, Jason was more of a follower, though he may have wanted to be the big guy among the other boys. Since Jason wasn't one to express himself. I was never quite sure what was going on in his head. There was still unrest in our home and some instances of behavior toward Jason that rattled me. There were certain situations when he would look at me with pleading eyes. There wasn't a lot I could do.

There was one time anger broke out between he and his dad in a gas station convenience store. It appeared it would become physical for a moment, then ended. Jason gave me that look. There was a time at the end of his eighth-grade year that his dad and I were called into the school principal's office because of something offensive and inappropriate Jason had written in a classmate's yearbook. I cannot remember what he'd written—except that I think he used foul language. I agreed it was tasteless and shouldn't have been written, but I did not agree with the intended punishment.

Again, Jason looked to me with those pleading eyes that cut right through me. It wasn't just his vulnerability, but my belief the punishment was beyond what was necessary. I forced my opinion and changed the outcome.

When Jason was fifteen, he needed his tonsils out. He'd been in some trouble, but getting his tonsils removed was not one of those times. I wondered if some of the drugs he'd used created the tonsil trouble, but I don't know. As he was wheeled away from me toward the operating room there were those pleading eyes again boring into me. I knew he was afraid but there was nothing I could do. I smiled at him, waved, and said, "I'll see you on the other side when you wake up." His eyes stayed on me until we couldn't see each other anymore. It's these moments of helplessness that still haunt me. By the time Jason had the tonsillectomy, I was no longer with his father. Divorce is a difficult journey. Yet I chose it and accepted all the consequences. One of these was not being in the same home with Jason as he recovered. I called every day. Even when his throat was too sore to speak, I could speak to him. My daughter came to live with me and her stepdad after a short time, but the boys didn't live with me again until later. They stayed in their schools.

I remember a phone call from Jason asking to come live with me and his stepdad. It was a very tumultuous time and trying to know the truth about anything outside of my own home was difficult. Jason was pleading. His father was telling me not to believe Jason and give into him. I didn't know who to believe or trust and was uncertain what decision to make. In the end, Jason did not move in with us.

Jason dropped out of high school for reasons I didn't fully know at the time. When I asked him for more detailed information while writing this book, he told me he left school because of gang activity. Gangs were, and I believe still are, very prevalent in the Central Valley of California. Jason was in a gang. He said his friends were being killed, and one day at school rival gang members came after him. He ran and saw a friend near her car motioning him to come. He jumped inside and she drove them away. After that day, he never went back to that high school again. If he had, he likely would have been killed. He went on to finish school at Dwight E. Furman High School, an alternative school offering independent study. He received his high school diploma through Furman. That was definitely an achievement, but things weren't getting any better. Jason continued down a treacherous path.

I didn't know when Jason's first experience with meth occurred. He recently told me he was fourteen when he first tried it. I was shocked! I didn't know who offered it to him, but he told me years later. A friend simply offered him meth and he said, "Okay". Why did Jason say okay? Why *would* he say okay? Why does anyone say okay? This is what my brain cannot process. Everything in me would run—run as fast as I could—away from such an offer, but the kids in our neighborhood seemed intent on trying drugs. I learned much later that drugs were easily available. There was a lot of drug abuse going on. Jason once told me that it took only one try and he was hooked on meth. At fourteen years old! Everything in me reacts to this with abhorrence. Unbeknownst to me at the time, my son was now hooked on meth and for years to come would seek this drug and others, leading him down a path of destruction.

5

ILLEGAL ACTIONS

Legal problems weren't far behind. One bad choice leads to another, especially when drugs are involved. Jason decided to forge a signature on some checks. I remember this being his dad's checks. Jason isn't sure. When it was discovered what he was doing, he was arrested. Rightly so, but it's an awful situation when you've committed a crime against your own parent. Drug users are desperate people ... desperate to get their fix any way they can. This means users will lie and steal from anyone. Anyone!

Since Jason was not living with me at this time, staying on top of all matters concerning him was difficult. I learned of this offense and his arrest and that he'd be going to court. Dreadful thoughts coursed through my mind. No mother wants to hear her son was arrested. He wasn't held in jail leading up to his court appearance, though uncertainty of Jason's future loomed heavily. The entire idea of Jason forging signatures, stealing, and going to court was gut-wrenching and how severe his sentence would be was worrisome. I tried to imagine myself visiting him in prison. It was a horrible thought and sadness enveloped me. My son in prison? My baby boy, my child, now a teen possibly going to prison? I couldn't fathom the possibility. Could it be real? Yes, it was his, and my, reality. My gut twisted painfully.

The court date arrived, and I drove to the county where Jason lived and where his trial would take place. It wasn't my first time being in a courtroom. I had been in family court multiple times. Never was one of those times pleasant, nor was this day to learn Jason's fate. That wasn't my last day in a courtroom, either. All these years later, I can say there isn't anything much more terrifying and unnerving than being in a courtroom, whether it's for yourself or someone else. Having a judge, who is a total stranger, rule over someone you care about is unsettling to say the least. And on that day, Jason would receive a ruling.

I sat in the courtroom waiting for Jason's turn before the judge. My hands sweated. I felt my heart beating faster than usual. I sat motionless while I squirmed inside—and I asked God for mercy for my son. Memories of Jason as a baby and as a small innocent child filled my thoughts. Then Jason's turn came and I strained to hear every word said by the attorney and the judge. I held my breath. What could be said? He was guilty of the crime.

Finally, the judge's words came and I released the breath I'd been holding. No jail time. No jail time! However, Jason was reprimanded and instructed to go straight to the jail where he would be booked and entered into the system the same as if he were being locked up. Then he would be let go through the usual release system. The no-nonsense judge sternly informed Jason that if he stole so much as a paperclip or stick of gum, he'd go straight to jail no if, ands, or buts and serve his sentence. I wondered if he took this to heart the way he needed to. I wondered if he would steal again.

I walked with Jason to the jail. I watched as he was escorted away, down the hall to a room I couldn't see, to be booked. I sat on a bench, nervous and relieved, and waited until he was released. As I sat there, I knew fully well that had the judge not shown leniency and given Jason a second chance, I'd be saying bye to him right then, and not to see him again until I visited him in prison. The thought sent a sickening shudder through me. No mother wants to have to visit her son in jail. Many sons would feel shame and discomfort having their mother come to see them in their orange jumpsuits. It's not an image I wanted in my head.

That was a heavy day filled with sorrow and despair. It was sobering for me and I believe for Jason, too. I was happy and relieved to see him released and off we went. I took him home to his dad's house. I drove to my own home shaken and wondered what would come next. Things still weren't resolved, and I knew it. It was difficult to put my finger on any one problem, but the underlying problem was drug use. No matter the reason anyone first tries a drug, if they are hooked the world turns on its side until the addiction can be beat.

6

Paintings on the Wall

Paintings can be beautiful—the colors and patterns and scenes. They are lovely in the right place on the right canvas or walls, but on the four walls of an apartment not so much. Apartment dwellers are normally not allowed to paint their walls in bright colors or murals. Every apartment is meant to be maintained for the next tenant—especially if you want your deposit back. I suppose most people follow the rules, at least generally.

Addicts don't think ahead or care much about consequences. They worry about it "later". I walked into Jason's nice apartment, located in a shade covered ground-level-only apartment complex. It was a nice place to live. Eventually all three of my children lived in the same complex at one time or another.

Jason was older now—old enough to work and have his own place. He had managed to stay out of jail and had his high school diploma. The time between his court case and moving into his apartment was filled with more drugs, trying to get through high school, his tonsils being taken out, and learning to drive. I was somewhat aware of his continued drug use and sketchy friends who also used. I had been to his school and seen his classroom, been with him at the hospital, and taught him to drive with the help of his stepfather. He was a good driver. He still is. I never saw him high when he was with us. Not drugged out of his mind, anyway. Since he did not live with me, I knew little of his daily life. He did act oddly at times, but not outright high. There must have been some low-level use that allowed him to function normally part of the time. Still, there was always something "off" that was intangible.

I went to visit Jason one afternoon at his new apartment. He was expecting me, but I wasn't expecting what I saw. His walls were covered in odd paintings—shapes and designs in a lot of bright colors. These were mostly abstract and some looked more like graffiti, but it was all very well done. This was the first time I realized Jason had some real talent for painting. This was all alien to me and I was shocked to see he'd used the walls as a canvas.

"Jason, are you allowed to paint the walls like this? Does your manager know? I asked.

"I don't know. Yeah, maybe, but I don't care. This is better than white walls." he said.

"I hope you don't get in trouble for doing this. You could lose your deposit, maybe even get evicted."

Jason didn't seem too worried, and he rarely complied with authority figures. Being a drug user, he didn't care much about anything but getting more drugs and getting high. With the knowledge I have now, I know smoking meth was his priority and that he was addicted.

I looked around Jason's apartment. It was typical for a teen his age, but the painted walls and images were unsettling.

During the writing of this book, Jason informed me that he and two friends would get high and paint the walls. His walls were the work of three. Three out of their minds on drugs. I've listened to music that caused me to wonder, *'Were they high or drunk when they wrote this song?'* Often that has been the case. So it was with these painted walls. Yes, they were high when they went overboard—even if much of it was lovely. There are songs and art that have gone down in history as some of the best that were done while the artists were high or drunk. The idea was, and is, unappealing to me. Day in and day out searching your next drink or fix and existing in a unstable mental state is sad, to say the least. To need to hide behind drugs, or self-medicate to feel better, to be absolutely addicted and at the mercy of dealers and mind-altering substances is heartbreaking beyond belief.

My heart was heavy as I left Jason's drug-damaged home. I wondered what he had in his possession that I knew nothing about. He was not going to subject his mother to the terror and darkness inside him. Even if I was aware of the problem, I would not know the details. I was at that apartment a few other times. Nothing had changed and the darkness in him terrified me.

There was only one thing to do. Pray. I had talked to God about Jason before. I had spent a lot of time talking to God about Jason and my other two children. I often asked for help and just as often thanked God for his help and provision. Talking to God was and is a daily activity for me—not only down on my knees but with every breath as I go through my days. At that time in Jason's life, I prayed more and more for him.

For decades I have been a fitness walker. During the time when Jason was living on his own, I prayed with every step I took. I remember walking and begging God not to let me hear that Jason was found dead from a drug overdose. I'd pray the same prayer the next day, and the next. Mothers cannot be with their children and make all their decisions for them. The time for mothers to tend twenty-four-seven ends early in a child's life. We teach them and train them to the best of our ability when they are young. We try to prepare them for life. Soon enough they start interacting with other children then go to school. We cannot be with them every minute or fix every incident that comes up.

Our children must face life—as scary and harmful as it can be—and fight their own battles. We cannot and should not protect them from every hardship or problem. They will become stronger facing these things on their own. It isn't that parents don't help and discipline their children, but some of that help is in letting them fall and face the consequences of their choices and actions so that they will learn. Mothers especially may struggle with this and want to make everything okay for their child, but it is a disservice to a child to overly protect them at any age. I heard the psychologist, Jordan B. Peterson, make this statement—paraphrased if not exact— *"Parents often spend too much time keeping the snakes away from their children, rather than equipping their children to be able to chop those snakes into pieces."* We mustn't overprotect them, and we so often cannot protect them.

What can we do? Pray. I continued to talk to God daily about Jason. I asked God to protect him from himself and his friends. I asked him to help Jason see the error of his ways and how he was hurting himself. Jason had a stubbornness within him at that time, that even if he wanted something good for himself, he would not choose it if he knew it'd make someone in authority happy. He continued to fight against authority. He carried some of that with him into early adulthood. I prayed for protection over him continually and I'd thanked God at the end of every prayer. This became even more constant as things worsened for Jason.

7

DARK DAYS

Jason was evicted from his apartment for not paying rent. I imagine rent money went to buying drugs. I'm sure he didn't get his deposit back. A drug user's life is always chaotic. A person cannot think clearly under the constant temptation and influence of damaging substances. It's a sad fact that some addicts abuse their brain for so long there is long-term or permanent damage.

Jason moved in with a friend older than himself. He was employed as a roofer by the father of friends of his. The roommate used angel dust—another name for PCP—as his drug of choice. Heavy-duty stuff. I don't know if Jason experimented with it, but his addiction to meth was ingrained. The mental picture I had of grown men living the drug life is a dark scene, but all too true—then and now. Drug and alcohol addiction is a disturbing situation. It's heartbreaking and extremely hard to deal with. It hurts individuals, families, and society. It ruins lives—period.

At some point during this time Jason took a job at a printing press across town. I was glad he was working. I mistakenly thought he was doing well enough if he was holding a job. I was wrong. It's amazing how my naiveness and hope hid much of what was truly happening. I couldn't know what was going on out of my sight and Jason was over eighteen. What a grown child does in his own home, on his own time, is far outside a mother's control. I believe mothers still wield some influence, if only a small amount, in the minds of their children. We spend years caring for and raising them. Surely, part of what we taught lingers somewhere in their psyches. Most assuredly my prayers had influenced Jason's life. I held fast to that truth.

I was home one day when I got a call that sent me reeling. It wasn't my worst-fear call. Jason hadn't Oded and died. It was his employer informing me that Jason was strongly under the influence of some substance, on the job, and they needed me to pick him up. The familiar stomach lurch, filled with butterflies and a bundle of nerves, immediately affected me. My heart pounded, my mouth went dry, I sweated. I had no idea what to expect when I'd see Jason. I'd never seen him noticeably high. I called my husband at work to tell him the situation and that I was on my way to pick up Jason. He insisted I come get him first. He would leave work and accompany me. Though I had no idea what to expect, he did, and he didn't want me going alone. That scared me. How would Jason behave? Meth is a stimulant. Would he be acting animated, silly, agitated, or maybe angry? If he was any of those, I would likely need my husband's help—even to get him into the car.

Looking back, I don't remember him being out of control. He was subdued and quiet. Maybe having his mother show up and take him home created more self-control. The ride was quiet. Once home, I remember Jason and I sitting on the stoop outside our front door talking—me doing most of it. Jason was in no shape to have a conversation. My husband and I spoke to him about staying with us. He was with us that day but went back to the place he was sharing with his older friend, for at least a week. It made sense since his clothing and other personal belongings were there. Afterward he did move in with us. He needed a safe place to live and a loving family around him. His younger sister was living at home, and since I worked from home, I was there, too.

We found it necessary to lay down some ground rules. Besides his younger sister, his three younger step-siblings were often over. For the health and safety of everyone, Jason was told there was to be no drug use, nor any drugs or drug paraphernalia in the house. This was a hard and fast rule and Jason agreed. Unaware of the full grasp that meth, or any of these hard-core substances had over addicts, I assumed he would easily break the habit and be done. ***In the dark*** is where I was. Even if he didn't use in our home, that wouldn't stop him from using elsewhere. Addicts never quit that easily.

8

ANGUISH

Jason got a new job at a pizza parlor and worked consistently. Again, I was fooled by his ability to hold a job. He seemed cheery around the house. We enjoyed having him with us. All the kids got along well enough. It seemed to me that things fell into a nice pattern, and I felt better being able to see him every day. He didn't have a car, so we drove him to and from work and other places.

I remember one day while giving him a lift, he confided something that had happened and hurt him deeply. I could hear the pain in his voice and see it in his face. He was brokenhearted in more ways than one. I assumed this had contributed to his drug use. I was surprised he'd shared his hurt with me, but happy that he did. He had allowed me into a part of his life and struggle. This was not without swearing me to secrecy. He did confide in me at times, often disturbing things, but I was happy that he did. I've kept these to myself. If they are to be told, it's his place to do so.

There was one memorable day, when Jason was in another part of town walking with his sister. He decided to jump, or do a flip, off a small wall. It wasn't very high, but he landed wrong and broke his ankle. I don't remember how the two of them got home, but it was obvious we needed to take Jason to the ER. I had an afternoon of piano students lined up, but my husband was able to take him. They had a long wait and had funny stories to tell about their experience sitting in the waiting room. When Jason was finally seen, it was confirmed his ankle was broken, and he was put in a cast up to his knee. He began the laborious task of wearing the cast and using crutches for at least six weeks, and I drove him to and from doctor's appointments to have his ankle checked. Fortunately, he was healing and managing.

We were all managing. The days were going by nicely ... or so I thought. There was a strange odor I would catch whiff of in the hall bathroom. On the counter was a bottle of men's cologne that belonged to Jason. I questioned him about the smell. He said it was his cologne and I wondered why he'd ever wear such an atrocious scent. I opened and smelled it myself but was uncertain if this was what I'd been smelling. This remained a mystery for me. Again, I had no idea what various drugs smelled like and little knowledge of which ones were smoked, injected, huffed, snuffed, swallowed, or any other way drugs are taken into the body.

While working on this book, I mentioned that mystery odor to Jason. I now know he was smoking meth in the bathroom. I didn't know. It's taken many years for me to learn certain facts.

One Sunday morning my husband and I returned from church and he became suspicious. He decided to immediately search Jason's room. I was taken aback by his need to do this and began feeling very nervous. My husband was not as naive as I was about drugs and addictive behavior. Jason wasn't home, if I remember correctly, or was outside. My husband found drug paraphernalia. We were disheartened and disappointed. I was shocked. It suggested there were drugs too, but this alone was a breach of the strict rules we'd set, to which Jason had agreed. My husband said, "Jason has to go. He broke the house rule." I knew. I understood what this meant. I agreed in my mind, but my heart was already breaking into pieces and bleeding all over my soul. Even so, we had to stick by our word.

That was it. Jason had to leave. Right away. I went into a quiet panic. Inside I was screaming, "NO!" I was his mom, and I was expected to tell him to pack his things and leave right away? I couldn't do it. I couldn't make my mouth move to speak those words, or any words. I was horrified about doing what we were about to do and was left utterly mute. I tried to speak, to tell my husband I couldn't say the words to Jason. My mouth and tongue refused to work properly. I believed we had to stick to the rules we'd set. I believed people young and grown must suffer the consequences for their decisions and actions, but I was overwhelmed with heartache. I had heart palpitations and physical pain. The emotional pain became so intense I was unable to speak or function.

Jason appeared and my husband managed to say the words I couldn't—that he must gather his things and walk out the door. He was told why and that he could not stay. It sounds harsh, and it was, but it was the only way to show we meant what we'd agreed to. There was no wiggle room with the drug rule. Jason muttered something about he'd simply forgotten the pipes and other things that he had in his trunk. It didn't matter. They were there and he must go.

I stood silent, feeling nothing less than terror. My head hurt, my throat ached, and tears streamed down my face as I watched Jason walk out the door—alone. We had just thrown my son out of our home with nowhere to go, no way to get anywhere, a cast on his leg, crutches, and his few belongings at his side. I've never experienced emotional pain as great as that day, with such strong reactions in my body. My mother's heart shrieked silently but hugely. It was a gut-wrenching split. My son was nineteen, but I felt as if my newborn baby was being torn from my arms never to be seen again. The anguish I felt was unbearable. I wondered what Jason must be feeling. His mother and stepfather – who both loved him – had thrown him to the streets! I cried harder and couldn't stop.

By God's grace, one good thing happened almost immediately. My other son and a friend of both the boys drove around the corner and saw Jason standing there at the curb. They talked with him then took him into their car and drove away. That small act on their part brought an inkling of peace to me. I knew they'd likely end up at the friend's house and I knew the mother well. It wasn't long before I got a call from the mother to tell me Jason was with them and he could stay a while. I breathed with relief that I knew where he was and was safe for the time being. Jason spoke to me on the phone as well. I don't remember what was said between us, but he was calm, and I felt the burden become just a slight bit lighter. He had a temporary home with a family I knew.

This fact did not stop my tears, however. I couldn't stop crying and I still could barely speak. I had no words. The emotion I felt disrupted all my senses. I continued the day in a stupor while continually crying. The night was long. I desperately needed help and counsel. Our entire family was upset, and we weren't in any shape to help each other. We all suffered greatly, but separately. I needed professional help to process the situation and calm me down.

Being a strong believer in God Almighty, I continued to pray for Jason, for me, and for all of us. There is a distinct peace that comes from turning to God and receiving his compassion and mercy. There is a hope that comes. I know this through my experiences and relationship with God and I never discount his help and power. This sustains me even in the darkest hours, but I sought earthly help as well.

I decided the next day to seek out pastoral counseling. I believed having a listening ear and counsel of a godly person independent of the situation could be helpful. I continued to cry nonstop and was exhausted when I walked into the office of the nearby church we'd been visiting. I was upset to the point that I could barely relate to the receptionist why I was there. She kindly listened to my few garbled words through uncontrollable sobs and went to speak to the pastor. He told her to send me in. I entered the pastor's office in the same shape as I was with his secretary. Sobbing to the point of not being able to catch my breath, he helped me calm down and gave me time to collect myself.

Finally, I told him the story that explained why I was so distraught. He listened closely and after I finished relating Jason's drug history and the time he was living with us, he sat very quietly then looked me in the eye and said, "You did the right thing." I sat in stunned silence with my tear-streaked face and tried to absorb what he'd just said. Suddenly, I felt the weight lift. Our decision to exile our son was accepted and advocated by this man of God. At that time "tough love" was a term often used in these types of cases, and he told me we had been courageous to utilize it with our son. He added that in the long run it may very well help him, rather than enable him.

For the first time in over twenty-four hours my tears dried up as I took his words to heart. I may have helped Jason, not destroyed him further. God himself spoke to me through this man who was doing his best to help a distraught and suffering mother. I went home feeling much lighter in my spirit and filled with new hope. I prayed constantly for Jason and for the circumstances in his life. My daily walks were filled with prayers for Jason's well-being and healing. I also prayed I would not get the dreaded call that he was dead. I watched and waited for positive signs and good news and a new and better life for Jason.

A family member once told me that Jason had said being kicked out was the best thing that ever happened to him. If so, maybe the pastor had been right, and we had helped Jason more than hurt him. I had the feeling that there were those who were appalled at our action to evict Jason. I also knew those people didn't know me or our situation well enough to judge. I ignored the negativity that came my way. Parents, especially mothers, are often judged by how they raise their children. In most cases, we'd be better off to mind our own children and households and let others mind theirs.

9

JASON'S DECISION

One day Jason showed up at our house and told me he'd made a decision. I inquired and he said, "I'm going into the Job Corps." I had heard of the Peace Corps but not the Job Corps. Jason explained it was for career training in various jobs. I learned that kids aged sixteen through twenty-four were eligible for free career training. He was eligible due to his age, low income, lack of focus, and other criteria. He had signed up and would be sent to Clearfield, Utah for his training. He'd be leaving soon. Overall, this sounded like a very good idea for him—the best reason because he had sought it out and chosen it himself. No authority figure was involved. That scenario made me happy.

The day Jason flew to Utah was an emotional one for me. I drove him to the airport. He was headed off into the unknown. I think it was frightening for both of us. This was especially difficult for me because I couldn't stay to see him all the way to the boarding area. That was a time when nonfliers could go past security and sit with their loved ones until they boarded, but I couldn't stay. Again, I had a lineup of piano students coming for the afternoon and it was close to the time my first student would be arriving. I was struggling with guilt at not being unable to stay and see him off. I was torn, but I said good-bye before he entered security and drove off leaving my son to an unknown future, alone. I cried all the way home.

The Job Corps offered free housing, nutritious meals, basic medical care, a living allowance, and career training. It was also run much like boot camp—strict! There were curfews with specific bed and wakeup times, room tidiness rules, mealtimes, and work hours. Phone calls and time off for holidays and home visits was limited. It was a two-year program, with much offered and much required, but beneficial to those who could stick it out.

Jason started training in operating a printing press, but soon discovered he'd rather be trained as a machinist. He switched and stayed in machining. Flash forward to the present, he stayed in that field and has worked as a machinist ever since—his entire adult life. Twenty-six years now in the field he trained for and rising to management positions. He is a success story.

Jason called home when allowed and let us know how he was doing. One day he told me he didn't think he was going to make it. He'd seen others thrown out of the program and thought it might happen to him, too. He was struggling to follow all the rules and submit to such authority. The rigor of school and obeying those in charge was tough but good for him, and he had a great opportunity to learn a life-long trade. I prayed he'd be able to live up to the rules and stick it out. I had no idea if he was using drugs during that time. I'm sure it wasn't allowed, but clever users can sneak things by many adults. Jason has since said that he could get any drug he wanted, and though he'd stayed sober for the first year, he did use drugs in the second year but never got caught or thrown out. Why would he start again? It's mind-boggling to me, but that's how addiction works.

One Christmas, Jason was home on leave and that was a joy. He enjoyed time away from the grind and we enjoyed having him around. Then he went back to Utah. Jason continued in his field and called home regularly. He managed to follow the rules well enough and was excelling in his work.

During one phone call, Jason told me he was entering a contest. The winner would receive $400, and a large toolbox filled with tools of the trade. I was excited for him, and I hoped and prayed he would win. It would do him so much good to come out the winner in his field. The phone rang one day, and Jason announced he had won. I was ecstatic! I believe to this day that this win was a huge self-esteem boost for him—something he desperately needed. He was a winner! He won prizes! I was a happy mom.

Time went by and Jason finished his time in the Job Corps. He'd had a big adventure away from home, in a state much different from California. He experienced winters with snowfall. Jason lived in a tough environment but stuck it out and saw it through. He gained a career and won a contest. He completed his two years and came back home to central California. He got a machining job in the San Francisco Bay Area and moved north. His dad was up in the area, as was his grandma. A new chapter began in Jason's life.

One day, a few months after Jason graduated, I received a call from the Job Corps. They were following up, as they do with all graduates. They were interested in how Jason was doing and if he was working in his field. I filled the man in and told him that, yes, Jason was working in the career they had taught him. The Job Corps is happy when they learn their part had been successful. About six months later I received another call checking in on Jason. I believe I received three calls in all. I appreciated their follow up. They were interested in everyone they'd helped and kept statistics on those who'd continued in their chosen field. Jason's decision to enter the Job Corps was a good one, and I would recommend it to others. They have 120 campuses nationwide and teach many trades that offer life-long careers.

10

LIVING ACCOMMODATIONS

Jason was working his full-time job in the Bay Area, but his life was still unsettled. I find it a miracle that he was able to hold a job, considering the drugs he used. It seemed more difficult for him to keep a home.

Jason first rented a room and shared the house with roommates. I felt relieved when I knew he had shelter. However, in this case there was a dangerous situation that occurred. Jason was home alone drinking and smoking. He passed out with a lit cigarette and his bed caught on fire. His roommates happened to arrive home right at that time, put the fire out and saved Jason's life. The house was saved from going up in flames. I believe he was asked to leave.

At one point Jason was living in a group home that housed both men and women. In recovery, men and women are told not to get involved in a relationship with another in the home, but Jason did. Eventually, the two of them shared an apartment and continued their addictions together. Neither was a good example for the other.

During this time, I traveled to visit Jason and his girlfriend for a few days. I stayed in their home on the couch. They took me to dinner to meet her parents that first night. It was a nice dinner and cordial. The next day Jason and I went hiking. We both enjoyed that day and have a funny story about me stumbling down a steep hill. My feet got away from me and I fell. The worst part was my brand-new tennis shoes were covered in dirt. I bought a second pair when I got home. I wasn't hurt and we had a good time. It seems a contradiction that we could have fun and laugh while he was still in the midst of addiction. I didn't see any drugs. I didn't observe him or his girlfriend using. I didn't see the effects of drug use, but there was still the feeling that all was not well. Things didn't add up. I know he hid his usage well from me. I was easy to hide it from, I'm sure.

Eventually Jason and the girl broke up. He lived alone in a series of apartments. I visited him a few times and saw several of them. All this time, he continued to work as a machinist. He changed companies once or twice but always stayed in the same career, and kept advancing.

Jason brought one girlfriend to our home. They came for a weekend but didn't stay at our house. By then we were living in a much smaller home than before and didn't have an extra room. They spent the nights with either his brother or sister. I remember the girlfriend. I knew little about her, but it was around Christmas time, and I wanted to give her a gift. I bought a package of cute slipper socks. She responded to the gift very positively and liked them. I remember that both of them really appreciated that I gave her a gift. I never saw her again, but their relationship lasted a while and was detrimental to Jason. As with the earlier relationship, they were both users and used together. This type of lifestyle is never good for either party.

Jason had been arrested for public intoxication and DUI's. Some of these happened in 2003 and 2004.

Again in 2011. Things were coming to a head. There was a lot of drug and alcohol abuse, the ever-present cigarettes, and a tumultuous relationship. I was told his girlfriend could be abusive, and neither she nor Jason were thinking clearly. How they both continued to work is a mystery to me.

It was around this time that my husband and I were going to move from California to North Dakota. When the day arrived the kids were there with us, including Jason, as the moving van was packed. We cleaned the house, had take-out lunch together, and visited until it was time for us to drive away. There was a major snag shortly after the movers arrived, concerning the cost of our move. We'd been quoted the price and agreed to the cost and all other conditions. We had our payment ready. Then the men who arrived to pack the truck told us it would cost more. They had not calculated the cost correctly due to the volume of our belongings. It was a lot more money and we were not prepared on that day. We discussed what to do—abort the entire moving day and try again, or find a way to handle the extra cost. Jason, realizing our predicament, approached us and offered to pay the extra expense. He was able and willing. After some discussion, we made an agreement with him to accept his money as a loan. He went to the bank. The movers were paid and continued packing. We set up a payment plan with Jason and paid him back. Even amidst Jason's addiction, he was able to hold a job, earn income, and help us in a pinch. We were grateful for his generosity. Later that day we were on our way.

Looking back, I'm not sure how I survived the good-bye. We were moving 1800 miles away for reasons that were not easy for others to understand. It would be a while before we saw family or friends again. I had told our kids that everyone was to leave before we drove away. We'd say our good-byes and they would drive away just like any other family get together. The thought of all of them standing there as we waved good-bye to each other was more than I could bear, and I didn't believe my daughter, or I, would handle it well. Once they had driven away, we put our dog in the car and drove off without looking back. We were headed toward our new home. The first night's stop was six hours away. It was a well-thought-out decision, and many positive out-comes were awaited.

Jason's addiction continued, however, and terrible things lay ahead.

11

The Calls

We'd settled quickly and easily into our North Dakota home. We called family often and sent pictures. We were happy and excited in our new environment. We found a house and jobs quickly. Having retired from teaching piano, I took a job at a local grocery store as a cashier. I often say it was the hardest job I've ever done. It was. There was more to learn than I could have imagined, and I stood eight hours a day. The job was like culture shock for me, having never done that type of work. In any case, I needed to work seven more years before I could retire, so I first took the cashier job, then nineteen months later I took a job in a bank as a receptionist and support person doing paperwork for two departments.

It was early in the cashier job that I received a disturbing call one morning just as I was about to leave for work. It was early fall.

Jason's girlfriend—the one I'd given socks—had found my number and called to ask if I'd heard from Jason. She had not seen him in two days. She couldn't locate him. He was missing. Terror struck my heart! Jason missing? Again? I finished my call and immediately started to contact the police in the city where Jason lived. I got nowhere fast and decided to call my daughter while hurrying to work. I had to be at my till in minutes. As a new employee, I didn't want to make waves. My daughter and I talked and decided she'd call around, including hospitals, and get back to me. Once at work, I told the office employees that I was expecting a call from my daughter due to a family emergency and asked they patch it through to my till. They agreed.

It wasn't long before I got the call I dreaded. Jason was in an Intensive Care Unit (ICU) with head trauma after his car hit a tree, head on. I assumed he'd been drunk. His injuries were serious, life threatening. My son had been in the ICU all alone with none of us aware. It was a sickening thought. My mother's heart cried out. His father wasn't too far away and if memory serves, went straight to the hospital. There are many times I've felt inadequate as a mother, but jumping on a plane right then was not an option for me and I managed with daily calls from my other two kids. Fortunately, Jason improved quickly and was released. I was relieved, but there was more trouble.

Jason went back home to the house with his unstable girlfriend. Once again ... no one under the influence of heavy drugs and alcohol functions well. Put two unstable people together and the equation spells disaster, no matter how nice or lovable they are. The girlfriend had been known to hit Jason and did so again, even hitting him on the head where his injury was still healing.

There was another incident. It was the Friday after Thanksgiving and my husband and I were standing in the frigid cold, our first winter in North Dakota, watching the annual Holiday Dazzle Parade. My cell phone rang. It was Jason. He was being admitted to the hospital. The doctors would need to drain his brain. *"What?"* Blood and fluids that normally would absorb back into the brain had not, and the pressure was giving him a terrible headache. The doctors were going to immediately start the process to drain the excess fluid. The news was disturbing, and we left the parade to go home and wait for more news.

It wasn't long before we received a photo of Jason sitting up in a hospital bed, fully awake, with a tube sticking out of his skull. It was a disconcerting photo, but he was doing all right. After the procedure, Jason went to his father's home to recuperate. His step-mother was a nurse, a handy person to have nearby. It was around this time that my other son gravely told me, that he didn't think Jason was going to make it ... meaning make it out alive from his drug addiction. It was sobering to hear and difficult to assimilate.

Prayer began, a mother's plea for her son's life. "Please Lord God, don't let me receive word of Jason's death. Watch over him. Help him. Save him. Help him make good choices."

Things began to change for Jason. As he explained ... he was having lunch with his girlfriend. She was crying and complaining. He suddenly had a "moment of clarity" as he put it, and realized he had a choice and needed to make some hard decisions. He broke up with her and walked away from that relationship. Both of us believe this was an intervention from God, showing that he could change his life.

Jason made arrangements to retrieve his belongings and enlisted the police to be at the location with him to ensure no battle or violence occurred. He had gained the knowledge and the strength to say his first "no" to his dire situation. It was the beginning of more good choices, though consequences from bad choices would follow him, and he'd have to answer to the law for his drunken accident—another DUI.

Much of what happened is a blur. I lived many states away. He moved into his own apartment. It wasn't easy to stay on top of Jason's activities. He had made his first good choice, but neither of us knew what lay ahead. He was still working, amazingly. I hoped and prayed.

12

CHOICES AND CHANGES

Jason recovered. About two weeks after his brain procedure, he began his life of sobriety. He let go of drugs and alcohol. Divine intervention, and the strength he found in it, saved him. At the time of this writing, Jason has been clean and sober eleven-and a-half years. The twelve-year mark is coming. Each one is a celebration. After twenty years of addiction, it was no small feat to rise above the hold that addictive substances can have and let them go—completely. The only substance that still had its clutches in Jason was nicotine. It took multiple tries before he finally conquered that addiction. As any smoker knows, cigarettes have a grip that can be harder to break than alcohol or drugs. Knowing how difficult it is for me to stick to only two eight-ounce cups of hot, dark cocoa

I enjoy daily, I cannot fathom the control of drug addiction and the strength of will it takes to overcome. It's inconceivable. Yet, Jason did it as others have also. It's not impossible. There is always hope.

Jason joined Alcoholics Anonymous (AA). He acknowledged and admitted his addiction and began the twelve-step program.

Jason began attending a local church. He liked the pastor and I'm sure he felt unjudged. It was different from the church in which he was raised and that was a positive for him. He went on a mission trip to El Niño, Baja California, in Tijuana Municipality, and built a house for a man and his daughter. He was baptized through that church there at Rosarito Beach.

He began helping in community programs that helped the less fortunate. He worked with Project 180, an organization that reaches out to the homeless. Jason worked with those who lived in the San Francisco Tenderloin, a forty-block neighborhood in downtown San Francisco. Homelessness is something he had experienced himself that is still troublesome to remember.

Jason also became a sponsor for a disadvantaged young girl and paid for her education. He supported her and her family.

Somewhere along his path of sobriety, he began speaking to AA groups and others. He worked in different mental wards, including Napa State Hospital. Jason gave his time and money to help others. This was surely part of his healing. Giving back is always positive. When we take our minds off ourselves and our troubles and focus on others, we have less time and energy to regress into negative thinking, old habits, and dangerous ways of living. Jason had walked in the shoes of those he spoke to and understood their struggles. When he spoke, he knew who he was talking to and what he was talking about. He also knew all the excuses addicts can give.

He found new activities such as running, biking, and swimming. Before long he was running marathons and participating in triathlons. He was mentally determined and became physically strong. For a person who'd struggled with asthma he was achieving beyond what I could have imagined. Jason set out to conquer fears and enjoy new adventures.

He skydived, hang glided, parasailed, floated the sky in a hot air balloon, hiked, rowed, took part in Spartan races, and more.

With drugs, alcohol, and cigarettes out of the picture, overcoming fear, engaging in more adventure, and better health were achievable. I have a framed collage Jason gave me filled with pictures of him doing many of these athletic activities. Jason took part in what are dangerous activities to me. A mother worries. One day I asked him not to tell me about them until they were over. I'd receive his call after-the-fact that he was alive and well. Some might say he traded one addiction for another, but what a better addiction—exercise and adventure rather than substance abuse. He's no longer engaged in those adventures but enjoys weightlifting and takes care of his body.

Jason began to excel in his work, which led to higher positions, and training and leading others. He's accountable and reliable. His bosses depended on him and elevated him to leadership. Jason has leadership skills. They might have once been buried, but no longer. Jason met his challenges head on and overcame. He is now Operations Manager. I imagine he could one day become Director of Operations.

While Jason was still going through the AA steps, he came home with us in June of 2013 after we had all attended his sister's wedding. My husband and I would be heading home the day after. Jason approached me in the evening after the ceremony and asked if he could come home with us for a two-week visit. He'd not seen North Dakota and wanted to visit us in our new home. The three-day drive would allow him to travel through states he hadn't seen. We agreed and welcomed him. Unbeknownst to us, he had another reason, too.

We had a fun drive home with Jason along. We stopped a few times for sightseeing and photos. We enjoyed the magnificent scenery of Nevada, Idaho, Montana, and then North Dakota as we drew closer to home. It was an enjoyable trip and nice visit—one I'll always remember.

One day, during his visit, while Jason and I were walking, he wanted to ask me a question. I said, "Okay". He asked if there was anything he needed to do to make up for the pain and suffering I'd experienced concerning his addiction and the consequences. I answered, "No, not a thing, just keep on doing good, and stay healthy and well." That's all I wanted. He didn't need to do anything to receive my forgiveness.

I found out afterwards that he was exercising step nine of the AA program and making restitution to those he'd hurt and affected negatively. He'd also approached my husband, his stepdad, with the same question and had received the exact answer I'd given him. We only wanted Jason healthy and well.

I know it must have been difficult for Jason to broach the subject and I imagine he'd been trying to find the courage to speak our entire walk … maybe for days. It takes courage to approach people you've injured and ask forgiveness, and also ask what can be done to rectify the situation and relationship. For me it was already rectified, and I saw no need for anything more. It was never about what he did to us, but what he was doing to himself and the horror that came with it. All was well between us, we assured him. He still had others he needed to approach, but that was up to him.

While Jason was visiting, he attended AA meetings. One meeting place is one street over from our house and an easy one-block walk. We attended the first meeting with him. He would receive a token of sobriety, and we wanted to be there. Since I've never used alcohol and had never been to an AA meeting, it was a little uncomfortable for me, only because I didn't relate, except for having watched Jason's addiction journey. We proudly sat with him, listened to everyone speak—others having achieved accomplishment, and some having fallen back. I felt for them in their struggles. With pride we watched Jason receive his token and celebrated with him. Every day was a new victory against addiction. Days of sobriety turned into weeks of sobriety, then months, and years.

13

RECOVERED

There are two thoughts about recovery. One is that a person is never recovered but always in recovery—that it's ongoing. The second is that a person has recovered—his addiction a thing of the past. It's over. I've come to believe both can be correct, depending on the person. I imagine addictive substances can be a life-long temptation for some. I know others who've ended their addiction, never to return, having lost all longing, need, want, or thought of it. In both cases, past users stay free of what once held onto them so tightly.

Jason has continued to stay free of substance addictions. He's been able to stick to the choice he made to change his life. He continued attending AA for a while. I believe he avoids people and places from his past. When we move on from an activity that's wrong or harmful, it's best if we avoid any precarious situations. This applies to everyone.

Jason has thrived in his work. Outside of his job he frequents the gym and engages in other activities he enjoys, including traveling. It is said that some people have addictive personalities and may be immersed and show 'addiction' in less harmful activities. For all of us, whatever we have a passion for and spend significant time doing could be called an addiction. The difference is if we can stop that activity or compulsion when needed and not be ruled by it. Jason has accomplished that.

Jason has friends and stays involved with family. He is an attentive son, grandson, and brother. He is continually generous with his time and money and helps in other ways. He makes the trek here once a year during the holidays. His sister and her family also live in North Dakota. He spends time with his brother and wife, his dad and stepmom, visits his ninety-eight-year-old grandma periodically, and talks with her daily.

Jason retains some of the stubbornness he exhibited in childhood, but he uses it in ways that serve him positively. He has a charm that draws people. He is free to spend his money on things other than drugs and free from the dangers of that life. He pays his bills. He's free of DUIs and jail sentences. I thank God his accident involved only himself and no one else was injured or killed.

Jason is a human being, and like the rest of us, whether we are, were, or have never been addicts, we must deal with the problems life throws at us. He's clear headed and able to manage. He's no longer a threat to himself. He is smart and capable. When the daily influence of mind-altering substances is gone a person can always function better. Part of Jason disappeared through those years when drugs ruled his life. We now have the complete person of Jason back. As he once told me, "It only took it once, and I was hooked on meth." I still don't understand that, but I believe it. It's happened to far too many boys and girls, sons and daughters, husbands and wives, men and women. Far too many are still stuck under the influence of drugs. Addiction happens quickly. Recovery can sometimes take a long time to reap the full benefits of being clean and sober.

Once free of addiction, clear-minded thinking can return, bodies can be healthy, relationships can be healed, former addicts can live full and meaningful lives. Happiness and joy can thrive in this new existence.

Recovery is the pot of gold, the gift, the blessing that awaits the one who decides to live substance free. Though the addict may not be able to achieve getting clean on his own, God is there to help simply for the asking. The addict must do the asking and take the steps. He must also accept the consequences of his previous actions.

Months after Jason's visit, he was arrested and served eleven days in jail for the DUI in 2012 when he wrecked his car and landed in the hospital with the head injury. The charges were dropped to a probation violation. Time had passed but he wasn't free from the consequences the law required. I was there when he stood before a judge after being arrested for writing bad checks, but I was far away from the arrests for public intoxication or any of the DUIs. In one way or another, Jason suffered the legal consequences of his choices and actions. At the time of his eleven-day incarceration he was already into the early days of his sobriety and working his way through the AA steps. He understood facing up to consequences.

Jason served his time, and moved on. Every day was and is a new day of sobriety. Aside from legal consequences, there are emotional, mental, physical, and relationship consequences to overcome. One day at a time, but with a new resolve, it can happen. It does happen. The hope we hold for our sons to be free of addiction is possible, but only they can make the decision and follow through.

AFTERWORD

This year on December 6th, 2024, Jason will celebrate twelve years of sobriety. This is an accomplishment! When I think about all that took place through the years, all I will never know, and the fierce grip that meth, alcohol, and cigarettes had over him, I am grateful for his life. It could have so easily ended differently.

I thank God for hearing and answering the prayers of a mother asking for her son's life. I thank God that Jason is one of his sons through faith. I thank God for holding onto Jason and for holding onto me as I struggled *in the dark*. There was so much I didn't know. Even with what I did know, I often didn't know what to do. There was much I didn't understand, and even when I did, I had little or no control. We cannot make decisions for others. We cannot make changes for others that only they can make for themselves. No matter how much we try to help and guide—sometimes succeeding and sometimes failing—the one thing that can remain consistent and make a difference is love and prayer. I loved Jason fiercely through every moment and struggle, and I prayed continually for him and for me, and all our family. Jason was loved by his entire family.

Jason made it. He is alive and well and active and working and involved with family. He is healthy. He made the choice to save himself. With God Almighty by his side, he succeeded.

I know this is not the outcome every mother has experienced. My heart aches for you if you are still engaged in this battle or have lost it.

Whatever the circumstances, we mothers love our children and yearn for their health and well-being. We hope and pray, but sometimes our children do not make the choices necessary or required to find their way out of the dark. We mothers suffer pain and sorrow, and often guilt. If you're a mother suffering guilt, realize so many of the circumstances are, or were, out of your control. Not your fault. Give yourself grace and forgive yourself for any mistakes you believe you made. Let it go. Give it all to God—every hurt, pain, sorrow, and guilt you feel. Accept his grace and forgiveness and let him carry you and your pain. The load will be much lighter. Have hope.

For decades after we made Jason leave our home, as written in the chapter *'Anguish'*, I could not talk about that time or tell the story without breaking down. Nothing has ever hurt me more. Eventually, I could talk about it with fewer tears. Recently, I spoke of that time with no tears. I wondered if I could write the chapter with no tears. I did. Healing has taken place. Just now, writing that sentence, "Healing has taken place", tears stung my eyes. Tears of joy and gratitude.

Something else brought new tears. Jason recently wrote saying, "I always tell people the reason I made it was because you were sober and always gave us so much love." Tears overflowed and ran down my cheeks. During all the years I stumbled around *in the dark*, never knowing if I was helping or hurting, being a decent mother or not, not knowing what to do or how to save Jason, he saw me as a beacon of love living an example of a sober lifestyle. I never realized. Even though our sons and daughters will make their own choices, our life example and love for them makes a difference. Believe it. I couldn't save Jason. It was out of my hands. Jason, along with his Father God's help, was saved from his life of addiction. His choices. His resolve. God had a plan for Jason—as he does every person.

These are my reflections on the years of Jason's addiction and recovery. It is my story and his story too, intertwined as it is with anyone close to an addict.

Never give up. Never lose hope. Never.
Nancy

www.nancykuykendall.com
email: nancy@nancykuykendall.com

"With man this is impossible, but with God all things are possible."- Matthew 19:26 NKJV

Other Books by Nancy Kuykendall

<u>NONFICTION</u>

Mornings on the Porch

Ordinary Wonders

Our Daily Moments

Now I Lay Me Down TO SLEEP – Help and Hope for the Sleepless

GOD IS NOT SILENT – One woman's encounters with God

Before God with An Open Heart – Daily Prayer

30 Days of Celebration – A Golden Collection

<u>FICTION</u>

THE OLD WOMAN series

Meet Rose - Book One

A New Year – Book Two

A Time of Change – Book Three

Full Circle – Book Four

<u>COLLABORATION</u>

Meandering: Essays and Short Stories by Jamestown Authors